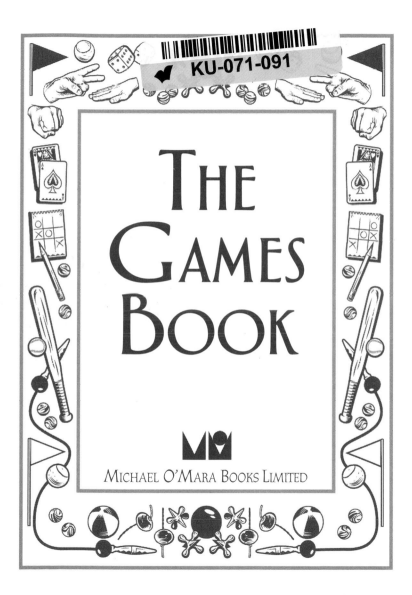

KU-071-091

THE GAMES BOOK

MICHAEL O'MARA BOOKS LIMITED

First published in Great Britain in 2008 by
Michael O'Mara Books Limited
9 Lion Yard, Tremadoc Road, London SW4 7NQ

Cover design by Zoe Quayle
Cover image by Paul Moran
Edited by Liz Scoggins

A CIP catalogue record for this book is available from the British Library.

Papers used by Michael O'Mara Books Limited are natural, recyclable products made
from wood grown in sustainable forests. The manufacturing processes conform to the
environmental regulations of the country of origin.

ISBN 978-1-84317-304-5

1 3 5 7 9 10 8 6 4 2

www.mombooks.com

Printed and bound in Finland by WS Bookwell, Juva

The publisher and author disclaim, as far
as is legally permissible, all liability for accidents,
injuries or loss that may occur as a result of the
information or instructions given in this book.

Exercise good common sense at all times; stay within the
law and local rules and be considerate of other people.

THE
GAMES
BOOK

Written by Huw Davies
Illustrated by Lisa Jackson

CONTENTS

Introduction	7	Adder's Nest	44
Deciders	8	Leapfrog	46
Dips	9	Hopscotch	48
Spuds	11	Elastics	50
Scissors, Paper, Stone	12	Double Dutch	52
Party Games	14	Clapping Games	54
Blind Man's Buff	15	Conkers	56
Hotter, Colder	17	Jacks	58
Wink Murder	19	Marbles	60
Dead Lions	21	Chasing and Hiding Games	61
Charades	22	Tag	62
Musical Chairs	26	Chain Tag	64
Simon Says	28	Stick in the Mud	66
Statues	30	Crusts And Crumbs	68
Musical Statues	31	Twos And Threes	70
Musical Bumps	31	Shadow Tag	71
Fanning the Kipper	32	Kiss Chase	71
Playground Games	34	Capture The Flag	72
British Bulldog	35	Hide And Seek	74
Red Rover	37	Sardines	75
Grandmother's Footsteps	38	Block	76
Follow My Leader	40	Word and Memory Game	77
What's The Time, Mr Wolf?	42	I Spy	78

Alphabet Minute	80
Fizz Buzz	82
I Went To Market	84
Kim's Game	86
Singing and Circle Games	87
The Farmer's In His Den	88
Oranges And Lemons	90
In And Out The Dusty Bluebells	93
Knots	95
Duck, Duck, Goose	96
Ball Games	97
Queenie	98
Kingy	100
Bad Eggs	102
French Cricket	104
Sevens	105
String, Cards and Paper Games	107
Cat's Cradle	108
Snap	111
Slapjack	112
Patience	113
Clock Patience	115
Rummy	116
Beetle	118
Consequences	119
Hangman	122
Noughts and Crosses	123
Nine Men's Morris	124

Introduction

The games described in this book will take you back in time, to an era in which children's television wasn't available morning, noon and night, there was no such thing as a computer game, and the Internet wasn't even a glimmer in its creator's eye.

This was a wild, lawless time, when children ran around in fields on long summer evenings – hiding, seeking, chasing and catching, staying out past tea time, bedtime even.

We hope this book will spark lots of happy memories, and also rekindle enthusiasm for all the games in danger of being drowned beneath the tide of the digital age.

Deciders

Before any game can begin there are decisions to be made.
Whether you need to choose who will be 'It', or who starts a
game, keep things fair using one of these 'deciders'.

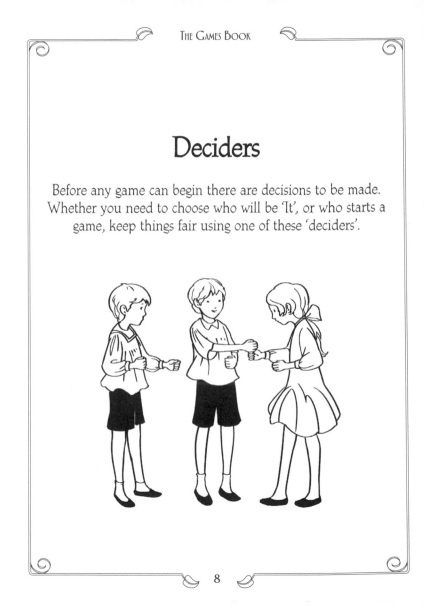

Dips

Dipping is a perfect way to cut out quarrels over who goes first. It uses a rhyme as a process of elimination and is a pleasantly long-winded game in itself.

Gather everyone who wants to play and, while reciting a rhyme, count round the group, one person per word. The person counted on the last word is eliminated.

Repeat the process until all but one are out, leaving one player to start the game. Here are a few rhymes to get you started:

> *Dip, dip, dip,*
> *My blue ship,*
> *Sailing on the water,*
> *Like a cup and saucer,*
> *Dip, dip, dip,*
> *You aren't It.*

Ip dip, sky blue,
Who's It? Not you.
Not because you're dirty,
Not because you're clean,
But because my mother says
You're the Fairy Queen.

Eeny, meeny, miny, mo
Catch a tiger by the toe,
If he squeals, let him go,
Eeny, meeny, miny, mo.

Two, four, six, eight,
Mary's at the cottage gate,
Eating cherries off a plate,
Two, four, six, eight.

Each, peach, pear, plum,
Out goes Tom Thumb.
Tom Thumb won't do,
Out goes Betty Blue.
Betty Blue won't go,
So out goes you.

Spuds

If everyone is fighting over who goes first shout, *'Spuds out!'*, then everyone gets in a circle, hands held out in fists, or 'spuds'.

Walk round the circle knocking on each spud in turn with one of yours, reciting as you go:

> *'One potato, two potato,*
> *Three potato, four,*
> *Five potato, six potato,*
> *Seven potato, MORE!'*

The spud knocked on *'MORE'* goes behind the player's back, and the count continues until all spuds but one are eliminated. The owner of that spud is It.

Remember to include your own spud in the count, knocking each on top of the other. If you are down to just one spud, count by knocking it against your chin (not too hard!).

Scissors, Paper, Stone
(Rock, Paper, Scissors)

Scissors, Paper, Stone is a great way of deciding who goes first or is It. It's also a very entertaining game. All you need are your hands, sharp wits and a worthy opponent.

How To Play

Facing one another, two players hold out a fist and use it to beat out the rhythm while chanting *'Scissors, Paper, Stone'*. Then each player shows one of these three shapes:

Scissors – The first two fingers extended.
Paper – The hand opened out flat.
Stone – A clenched fist.

The aim is to choose a shape that beats your opponent's.

Paper beats stone – because paper can wrap a stone up.
Stone beats scissors – because scissors can't cut stone.
Scissors beats paper – because scissors can cut paper.

If you both choose the same shape, it's a tie, and you must try again.

Play a single challenge if you need a quick decision, or 'best of three' or 'best of five'.

Tactical Tip

Cheating is possible – a player can delay their shape until the last moment when they have seen their opponent's. Deal with cheats by having players make the shape behind their backs then show them at the same time.

Party Games

Perfect for making any child's party go with a traditional 'bang', this selection of party classics will keep your guests busy for hours (and help burn off that jelly and cake).

Blind Man's Buff
(Blind Man's Bluff or Pickety Witch)

A party favourite, *Blind Man's Buff* has been played for hundreds of years. It works well with at least six players, depending on the size of the room you are playing in. This game is sure to wear out even the most energetic guests.

How To Play

In the classic version of *Blind Man's Buff,* one person is blindfolded and spun around three times by the other players until they are disorientated. The Blind Man then moves around the room, with his hands outstretched and attempts to tag the other players. The other players bolt around the room keeping out of the Blind Man's reach as long as possible. The last person to be tagged is the winner.

Variations

Players can remain stationary, either seated or standing, while the Blind Man seeks them out. They are allowed to bend and twist out of his reach, but they cannot actually move from the spot.

In another version, the Blind Man has to try and guess who they have in their grasp. They can use their hands to feel the person's features. If they succeed they can hand over the blindfold, if they fail they carry on trying to tag people.

Tactical Tips

If you are the Blind Man, remember to use your other senses to help you hunt players down – the sound of someone giggling or a waft of air as someone brushes past you will help enormously.

Whichever version of the game you decide to play it's best to keep doors shut and clear the room of any clutter before you start, to avoid injuring the Blind Man.

Hotter, Colder
(Hunt The Thimble or Hunt The Slipper)

Perfect for a traditional party, *Hotter, Colder* is a hiding and hunting game, played indoors.

How To Play

Select a small household object – anything from a pencil to a button is perfect. One player, the Hunter, leaves the room for a minute, while the other players decide on a hiding place for the chosen object.

The Hunter is allowed back into the room and starts to hunt down the object. The only clues the other players can give are *'Hotter'* the nearer the Hunter gets to the object, or *'Colder'* if they move away from it. If the Hunter gets very close, they can shout *'Burning'*, and if the Hunter is completely off course, they can shout *'Freezing'*.

When the object is found, another player leaves the room and the object is hidden again.

The difficulty of this game depends on the size of the object hunted and the area in which it's hidden – this can be varied according to the age and ability of the players.

If the object is too small and difficult to find, or there are too many obscure hiding places, the game can go on for ages. Why not add spice by having a time limit on searches?

Reverse Rule

A variation of this game is to have many Hunters. One player hides the object while all the others are out of the room. When the Hunters return, they are directed with a shout of *'Hotter'* or *'Colder'* until someone succeeds in finding it.

Wink Murder

Wink Murder is a game of cunning and trickery. It requires a minimum of five players, and is perfect to play around the dinner table.

How To Play

Tear off a piece of paper for each person. Mark one with a cross and leave the rest blank. Scrunch each of them up into a ball and pop them in a hat or bowl.

Offer the hat around for each player to take a paper ball. Players must open out their paper ball discreetly. One person will find they have the cross – this means they will play the part of the 'Murderer'. Everyone else is both a potential victim and a detective.

The aim for the Murderer is to 'kill' all the players around the table without getting caught. To kill someone, the Murderer must catch their eye and subtly wink at them without the other players noticing.

The aim for the other players is to identify the Murderer before they become victims.

The game begins, and everyone around the table must look at each other in turn, making eye contact. The Murderer strikes and his victims use their acting skills to full effect as they keel over and die a dramatic death.

Anyone who thinks they have worked out who the Murderer is can formally accuse them. But if they are incorrect they will be punished with death!

A variation can be played with a designated 'Detective' who sits among the murder victims. If the Detective successfully identifies who the killer is before everyone is dead, the Murderer becomes the next Detective. If not, they remain Detective for the next game.

Tactical Tip

If you are the Murderer, take your time picking off your victims. Don't begin with the people directly opposite, since that will make you a prime suspect.

Dead Lions
(Sleeping Lions)

Perfect for any moment when noise and excitement levels have reached a peak, *Dead Lions* is a parental party favourite. Simply get all the players to lie on their backs on the floor and compete to be the stillest, quietest 'Lion' of all.

If asked to keep their eyes shut, some may even fall asleep.

Now, tiptoe away and start the tidying up.

Charades

This classic play-acting game is great fun at family gatherings, when a normally serious aunt or uncle can have everyone in stitches. A minimum of four players is required.

How To Play

Divide into two teams and give each team a bowl and a pencil and paper.

Out of your opponents' earshot, choose a selection of titles from television, films, plays, books, musicals or songs. Well-known phrases or famous quotations are also allowed. Write each of the titles down on a separate scrap of paper, fold them up and pop them in your bowl.

Select a team to go first and a member of that team to be the first mime artist. The mime artist picks a title from the other team's bowl and reads it to themself. The player's task is to communicate the title picked to the rest of their team using nothing but mime. No props or noises are allowed.

A time limit is agreed for each turn – say two minutes – and a timer or watch is used to enforce the limit.

Mime Time

The mime artist starts by describing the type of title they have picked. Here are the established mimes for each genre:

Television – Draw a rectangle in the air with your fingers.

Film – Pretend to crank an old-fashioned movie camera.

Play – Draw both hands apart, as if opening stage curtains.

Book – Palms together, open them up like a book.

Musical – Go down on one knee with one arm held out dramatically.

Song – Cup hands around open mouth to indicate singing a song.

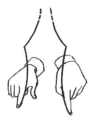

Phrase or Quotation – Use index fingers to draw inverted commas in the air.

Word Count

Next, the mime artist shows how many words are in the title by holding up the correct number of fingers. Alternatively they can sweep their arms in a wide circle to show they are going to act out the whole thing without breaking it into individual words.

If the mime artist breaks the title into individual words, they hold up their fingers to specify which word they will be attempting. They can even break a word up into syllables to make it easier to guess. To show the number of syllables in a

word, they hold the appropriate number of fingers against one forearm, then do the same to indicate which of the syllables they are miming first.

For any small words in the title, such as 'a', 'it' or 'of', the mime artist should hold a thumb and forefinger close together to show a small size.

If a word is difficult to convey, but an easier word sounds similar, a tug of the earlobe indicates 'sounds like'.

Getting It Right

When a member of their team guesses a word accurately, the mime artist taps his nose and points straight at the person who guessed correctly.

If the whole title is guessed in time, the team wins a point. If they run out of time, or only guess part of the title, they do not score. In both cases, play passes to the opposing team.

Tactical Tip

Ensure the titles you write down for the opposing team are as difficult to mime as possible.

Musical Chairs

This classic party game is usually played by children, but sometimes grown-ups can't resist joining in. You will need several chairs – one fewer than there are participants – and a source of music, such as a CD player or piano.

How To Play

The chairs are arranged in two columns, back to back with the seats facing out. One person is in charge of the music.

When the music starts, everyone walks, or dances, in a line around the chairs. The musical controller or pianist stops the music at random, and everyone must sit down as quickly as they can, leaving one person without a chair.

That person is out of the game. A chair is removed, and the game begins again.

In each round the last player to reach a chair is out, until there is just one player left victorious.

A Variation

If space allows, a good alternative is to arrange the chairs in a circle or a square, with one chair per person. Everyone dances in a line, moving clockwise around the chairs.

In this version, each player must remember which chair was theirs originally. When the music stops, everyone races back to their own chair by continuing in a clockwise direction. The last person to sit down is eliminated and their chair is taken away.

Simon Says

Simon Says is a timeless party game that can be played with large or small numbers of people.

How To Play

Decide which person will be Simon. Simon stands in front of the other players, and tells them to perform certain actions, such as jumping in the air, touching their noses, turning around, wiggling their fingers, shouting *'Hello!'* and so on. The actions can be anything Simon thinks of – so long as everyone playing is capable of doing them.

The key to the game is whether Simon adds the words *'Simon says...'* before an instruction or not.

If Simon says, *'Simon says wiggle your fingers'* – then everyone must wiggle their fingers. If Simon just says *'Wiggle your fingers'*, no one must wiggle their fingers. Anyone not paying attention who does wiggle is out.

The last player not to be knocked out wins. The winner can be presented with a prize or play the part of Simon in the next round.

Tactical Tips

Simon can trick players into making mistakes. He could say *'Simon says raise your left arm,'* while raising his right arm. Alternatively, he could disguise a command, for example, *'Can someone go and see if Mum's in the living room?'*

Statues

A game of balance and control, *Statues* challenges everyone's ability to think quickly and keep their footing.

How To Play

For the simplest game of *Statues* a player is chosen to be 'It' and the rest become human statues.

To start, It turns away. The statues then run, jump, prance and dance about as much as they like. However, It can turn around at any time, and all the statues must freeze immediately in whatever position they find themselves at that moment.

It can walk around among the statues to check that no one moves a muscle. Anyone who does is out of the game.

To restart play, It shouts *'Go'* and turns away again. The winner is the last person to be caught moving.

Musical Statues

To turn *Statues* into *Musical Statues,* simply add music. The
person chosen to be It gets to control the music.

The statues dance around until It suddenly stops the music.
They must then come to a complete standstill. Any player
caught wobbling is out. Then the music resumes – last
person standing is the winner.

Musical Bumps

Musical Bumps is an ideal
alternative for more robust
competitors who don't mind
tumbling to the floor.

Instead of having to freeze in an
awkward position when the music
stops, players must sit down on
the ground as quickly as they can.

The last player to sit down is out.

Fanning the Kipper

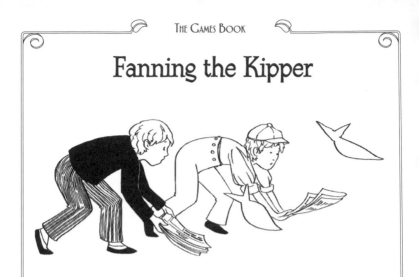

Fanning The Kipper is a race, so the more players the merrier, depending on the space available. It is strictly an indoor game, since any breath of wind could spell disaster. Any adult who would rather not take part can volunteer to set the course and act as an umpire.

How To Play

Each competitor needs a folded newspaper to fan with and a 'kipper' made out of a piece of tissue paper 20 cm by 10 cm, cut into the shape of a fish.

While everyone is cutting out their kippers, the umpire should decide on a course. A route straight across a room is

simplest, since fanning in a straight line is easiest. For more skilful players a demanding course, moving from room to room, can be devised. Just be sure to remove any breakables to a safe place.

Start Fanning

When everything is set, players line up, placing their kippers on the floor in front of them. On the word 'Go', they use their folded newspapers to fan their kipper forward.

The first player to complete the course is the winner.

Playground Games

Lunches and break times have never been so
much fun – use all your cunning and co-ordination
to get the most out of free time and open spaces.

British Bulldog

British Bulldog is a game that adults always have fond memories of playing, yet would rather their own children don't try. That's probably because it can get a bit rowdy. For this reason it is a game best played on sand or grass rather than a less forgiving school playground. Younger children should probably just watch.

How To Play

In an open space, mark out two safe zones, roughly eight metres wide and between six and eight metres apart. A 'Catcher' is chosen who stands in the 'danger' zone between the two safe zones. All the other players form a line inside one of the safety zones.

Then as one, the group have to rush across the danger zone to the other safe area, trying to avoid the Catcher. The Catcher, however, tries to grab a player, and hold them down on the ground or lift them off the ground for a count of ten, or while saying *'British Bulldog, One, Two, Three'*. Any player successfully captured joins the Catcher against the main group.

The game continues, with the number of Catchers gradually increasing against fewer and fewer players in the safe zones.

At this point rough-housing often erupts as survivors desperately bid to be the last player standing and therefore the winner.

Tactical Tip

When you are Catcher, concentrate on the smallest players first. Then you'll be able to work as a team to catch bigger, stronger players who, in turn, will be able to capture other people solo.

Red Rover

Red Rover is a game of strength, played between two teams.
Unlike *British Bulldog*, a soft surface isn't strictly necessary.

How To Play

Divide into two teams. One is the 'chain' and links hands,
facing the other team about four metres away. The chain
team challenges a member of the other team – chanting:

> 'Red Rover, Red Rover,
> We call [David] over!'

David charges at the chain, trying to
break through. If he succeeds, his
team can pick a player from the
chain to join their team. If he fails,
he has to join the chain. The winner
is the last person 'free'.

Tactical Tip

Challenge smaller players. They
are unlikely to break through your
chain and will be obliged to join
your team.

Grandmother's Footsteps
(Peep Behind The Curtain)

Any number of players can join in with this playground favourite — as long as you have enough open space. One child acts as 'Grandmother', while the rest sneak up behind her, hoping to reach her before she can spot them moving.

How To Play

Select a player to be Grandmother then stand in a line, several metres behind her. As soon as she turns her back to the other players, they must start trying to creep up on her and touch her on the shoulder.

Grandmother can turn around at any time without warning and players must freeze instantly. If she spots anyone moving, they are sent back to the starting point. The first person to tap her on the shoulder becomes Grandmother.

To give the players enough time to

get moving, Grandmother must recite a rhyme under her breath such as:

'L-O-N-D-O-N spells London...'

Or, count to ten quietly. There is no restriction on the speed she counts, so watch out!

Tactical Tips

Your triumph will depend more on the strategy you choose, plus a bit of luck, than your speed and strength. Inching forward, as slowly as possible, means that you'll be much harder to catch out, but you'll take a long time to get anywhere near Grandmother. Rushing to cover as much ground as you can is a gamble on being able to stop quickly enough when she suddenly turns around. Either way, it's vital to keep a close watch on Grandmother for any signs that she might spin around and spot movement.

Follow My Leader

At its most extreme this game can become a route march across fields and woods, with the 'Leader' taking followers into all sorts of tricky spots. At its most basic it is a simple party game that all small children can enjoy.

How To Play

Choose one player to be the Leader – often this will be the boy or girl with the most energy, or the person that everyone else considers most intrepid.

The Leader sets off walking, with all the other players in a line behind. The Leader can go anywhere and carry out any actions – a whistle, a shout, a jump, a cartwheel, a funny dance, and so on – and the followers must copy exactly. If they don't, they are out of the game.

The Leader must test the abilities of the followers as much as possible and this is what makes the game fun. Don't get carried away and land anyone in hospital!

The game continues until all the followers refuse to do something, give up and drop out. If the Leader starts to get tired, a replacement can step in at any time.

What's The Time, Mr Wolf?
(What's The Time, Mr Fox?)

A gloriously simple yet suspenseful game of chase that is always extremely popular with children, *What's The Time, Mr Wolf?* can be played almost anywhere, as long as there is a reasonable amount of space to walk and run in.

How To Play

Choose a starting point that will also be the 'safe' area to return to when the chase is on. 'Mr Wolf' is selected and walks away from the rest of the players in a straight line, while they follow.

The followers regularly call out 'What's the time, Mr Wolf?' and Mr Wolf replies by saying 'Nine o'clock', 'Five o'clock', or any other randomly chosen time.

Each time the followers ask 'What's the time, Mr Wolf?' they should dare themselves to get nearer. The Wolf will be able to tell by the sound of their voices how close they might be. When he thinks he might be able to catch one of them, he'll wait to be asked the time again, then turn unexpectedly, growling 'Dinner Time!' and chase everyone back to the safe area. Whoever is caught becomes the next Wolf.

Tactical Tips

If you are following Mr Wolf try not to give away your location by shouting out the question any louder than the other players. Also, noisy feet will have Mr Wolf on to you very swiftly.

Adder's Nest

Adder's Nest is an old game that makes a great test of strength and guile – all you need is a central object to represent a nest, such as a drain or manhole cover. Oh, and strong arms are a must.

How To Play

Players make a circle of five or six people around the nest. Each player hooks their hands together with the people either side of them. The circle gathers as close to the nest as possible and chants:

> *'Five little sausages frying in a pan,*
> *One went pop and the others went BANG!'*

On *'BANG!'* everyone jumps back from the nest and the battle begins, as players attempt to pull one of the other players onto the nest and keep themselves as far from it as possible.

Anyone who touches the nest is 'poisoned' and out of the game, but this only counts if the circle was not broken at the time.

The game continues with a smaller circle each time until just two players remain, fighting it out to be the winner.

Tactical Tip

If a player next to you seems particularly strong, try to outwit them by allowing them to take you as close to the nest as you dare before attempting to tug them across it instead at the last moment.

Leapfrog

It is possible to play *Leapfrog* with just two players, but larger numbers will make for much more fun. *Leapfrog* can be played virtually anywhere, but soft grass is an advantage.

How To Play

All the participants line up and 'make a back' – placing their hands firmly on their thighs, feet apart for balance and head tucked well down.

The person at the back of the line is the first 'Leaper'. The Leaper takes a short run-up, puts their hands evenly on the first back and leapfrogs over. They leap over each player in the line, then run forward a few paces and make a back themself. At the same time the person who is now at the back of the line begins leapfrogging.

The game continues until everyone has both leaped and been leapfrogged over.

When the first Leaper is back at the end of the line, they try to jump over all the people in front again.

The aim is to keep the chain of leapfroggers going without everything turning into chaos.

The pressure is on for players to regain their balance and form a back quickly after leaping. This way they can avoid ending up on the floor when the next leapfrogger arrives.

Round And Round

Try *Circle Leapfrog*, with one person leaping round and around until they give up and drop out.

You can be as inventive as you like with *Leapfrog*, so add as many variations as you wish.

Hopscotch

Hopscotch can be played anywhere that you can chalk out the classic layout. It can even be adapted to the pattern of paving slabs where you live.

How To Play

The most common layout used to play *Hopscotch* today is squares — alternately one square then two, finishing with a single square to make a total of ten.

Draw the layout of the *Hopscotch* pattern, either by chalking it onto the ground, or by marking it out in sand or dirt with a stick.

Number the squares one to ten with your chalk or stick.

To start, throw a small pebble on to square 1. Make sure the pebble lands cleanly inside the box – if it lands touching a line your turn is already over.

Jump over the square containing your pebble, landing with your left foot in the 2 square and your right in 3. Continue, alternately hopping and jumping until you reach square 10. Then turn (balancing on one foot) to make your way back to your pebble. Stop on squares 2 and 3 to pick the pebble up before jumping over square 1 to complete the course.

If you touch a line with your foot, lose your balance, or miss a square, your turn is over. When it comes back to your turn you have to start from square 1 again.

Each time you successfully finish the course, throw your pebble to the next square in sequence. So your next throw would be into square 2. Hop on your left foot through squares 1, 3 and 4.

Tactical Tips

It's best to find an odd-shaped stone, with a flat side which will not roll, and practise accurate throwing skills first.

Elastics

(French Skipping or Chinese Jump Rope)

Elastics is a highly skilled jumping game which spread like wildfire on its arrival in Britain in the 1960s.

How To Play

Tie a length of thin elastic about three metres long, into a loop. Two 'Enders' stand, facing each other, inside the loop and hold the elastic taut around their ankles. The third person must attempt to perform a sequence of jumps.

At a pinch you can stretch the elastic around the legs of two chairs and play solo if you want to practise by yourself.

Chant a rhyme while you jump to keep momentum:

> 'England, Ireland, Scotland, Wales
> Inside, outside, puppy dog tails!'

> 'Jelly on a plate
> Jelly on a plate
> Wibble wobble, wibble wobble
> Jelly on a plate.'

- Jump into the middle of the elastics facing one Ender.
- Jump so that each foot lands on a strand of elastic.
- Next, jump one foot in the middle, one outside the elastic.
- Turn and repeat before jumping into the middle again.
- Now jump so that your feet land either side of the elastic.
- Hook each elastic with your toes and cross your legs over.
- Release with a scissor kick then land in the middle again.
- Jump out to one side, facing the elastic.
- Hooking the first strand with your toes, jump across to the other side, making a diamond shape.
- Lastly, jump all the way out to one side in a graceful finish.

If successful, the Enders raise the elastic to knee level, then thighs, then waist, making each round more difficult. If you miss a jump, you're out, and one of the Enders takes a turn.

Double Dutch

These days, *Double Dutch* skipping has become a competitive sport, but it's just as good with a couple of friends and some music. You'll need practice to get it right, but once you do it's great fun and excellent exercise, too.

How To Play

Double Dutch uses two long ropes swung in opposite directions (special *Double Dutch* ropes are available).

You'll need two 'Enders' with strong enough arms to keep the ropes turning. This can be tricky at first, as it requires good co-ordination and some practice.

The Enders stand two to three metres apart, take a rope in each hand and turn them alternately in large arcs. Their left hands should rotate the rope clockwise, and their right hands should rotate the rope anti-clockwise.

Once a steady rhythm is established, it's time for the skippers to jump in. The first stands beside one of the Enders and watches the ropes for a few moments. They should wait for a 'window' to open up between the ropes when the nearest rope is on a downwards swing, before trying to hop over it. They should then hop in on a diagonal and start jumping immediately!

Practice Makes Perfect

Start with simple two-footed jumps and skipping from foot to foot. Then practise turning around on the spot or hopping. Take turns so everyone has a go at skipping and being Enders.

Tactical Tip

Practise keeping a good rhythm going with a song or chant.

Clapping Games
(Patty-cake)

Clapping games are perfect to play in pairs, or for several children sitting in a circle, clapping in time to a song.

How To Play

Face your partner, a little way apart, and clap hands in sequence, mirroring one another's actions.

- Clap your hands together, then clap both palms to your partner's palms.
- Clap hands, then clap your right hand to your partner's right hand, diagonally.
- Clap hands, then left hand to left hand, diagonally.
- Clap hands, then clap both hands to your partner's again.
- Repeat, with double claps.

When you've built up confidence add in some extras:

- Clap both hands on your thighs.
- Clap your shoulders, knees and toes.
- Bring your right hand down and your left hand up, clapping hands as your partner does the same.
- And reverse!

Build up a rhythm to one of these classic clapping rhymes:

> *A sailor went to sea, sea, sea,*
> *To see what he could see, see, see*
> *But all that he could see, see, see*
> *Was the bottom of the deep blue sea, sea, sea.*

> *Three, six, nine, the goose drank wine*
> *The monkey chewed tobacco on the street car line,*
> *The line broke, the monkey got choked*
> *And they all went to heaven in a little row boat.*

Try to sing and clap faster and faster and carry on for as long as possible without making any mistakes.

Conkers

In autumn, when the fruit of the horse-chestnut tree ripens and falls to the ground, there's nothing like a game of *Conkers*. Even though the game is no longer welcome in some school playgrounds, you can still go 'conkering' in your local park.

How To Play

Make a hole through the centre of your conker with a skewer (this is a job for an adult). Take a shoelace or a piece of string about half a metre long and tie a firm knot in one end. Thread the conker onto the shoelace. Let half its length hang from your hand, with the rest of the lace wrapped around your fist.

To claim first hit, be the first to say:

'Obbly, obbly onker, my first conker.'

To get a good hard hit, hold the string in your strong hand, with the conker gripped behind two fingers of the other hand. Stretch the string out tight, almost as if you were shooting an arrow from a bow.

Take aim at your opponent's conker, release the conker from behind your fingers as you pull forwards and down with the hand holding the string.

Take turns to hit each other's conker or allow each player three attempts to strike before swapping over.

If the strings tangle, the first player to say *'Strings'* gets another shot.

The game ends when a conker breaks or starts to disintegrate.

Give your winning conker a name matching the number of other conkers it has destroyed. It will be a 'Twoer', if it beats two conkers, but if a Twoer beats a Fiver add the victories of the beaten conker and call it a Sevener.

Tactical Tips

A hard conker will beat a softer conker. There are ways of ensuring that yours is almost unbeatable. A good soak in vinegar or baking in the oven will harden a conker, but these methods are frowned upon. Instead, just put some conkers into a bowl of water. Any that sink are denser and stronger. Discard the ones that float on the surface.

Jacks
(Fivestones or Knucklebones)

Jacks is an ancient game, which was once played with real animal bones, later with pottery, wood or ivory pieces. Modern jacks are mass-produced, six-pointed metal shapes, usually sold with a rubber ball.

How To Play

You'll need a pack of ten jacks with a ball and someone to play against.

To start, throw the ball up in the air and pick up a jack from the ground with your throwing hand. Then try to catch the ball with the same hand before it bounces.

Repeat this move until you have picked up, and put aside, each jack once. This is known as Onesy.

Next try to pick up five lots of two jacks for Twosy, three lots of three and a single jack for Threesy, two lots of four and the remaining pair for Foursy and finally, two lots of five for Fivesy.

When you miss, your opponent takes a turn.

If you are struggling, give yourself extra time to pick up the jacks by adding a bounce before you catch the ball.

Challenging Combinations

As you improve at *Jacks*, add challenging combinations, such as clapping while the ball is in the air before you scoop up any jacks.

Traditionally the last, and hardest, *Jacks* combination is called 'Everlastings'. Throw all the jacks up into the air in one go. Immediately turn your hand over and attempt to catch all of the jacks on the back of your hand.

Next, fling the jacks up from the back of your hand, picking up any that fell to the ground in the first place, before catching the rest safely in your palm. This takes some practice.

Tactical Tips

On the earlier levels of a game of *Jacks*, throw the jacks so that they are scattered over a wide area. This makes it easier to pick up just one or two.

On higher levels, use a more gentle throw to keep the jacks closer together and make it easier to grab several at once.

Marbles

Marbles has been played all over the world for thousands of years in various forms.

Marble Technique

The usual technique of propelling a marble is known as 'Knuckling'. Hook the marble in your index finger, with the knuckle resting on the ground. Flick the marble with your thumb.

'Lagging' is a way of choosing who goes first: each player rolls a marble towards an agreed target. The one whose marble is closest has first go.

Ring Marbles

A classic game of 'Ringy' or 'Ring Taw' Marbles is played in a circle, roughly 20 cm wide, marked out on flat ground. Each competitor places a marble in the ring. The players flick a marble towards the circle, aiming to knock out their opponent's marble. If successful, they can claim the marble. To keep things fair, it is a good idea to mark a second circle around the first as a shooting line.

Chasing and Hiding Games

There's nothing like a simple game of *Tag* or
Hide And Seek to while away long afternoons and
wear you out before tea time.

Tag
(Tig, Tiggy, Tick, Ticky, Touch, Had, Chase, Catch or Dobby)

Nothing quite matches the simple spontaneity of a game of *Tag* in the playground or at a picnic.

How To Play

All you need to play is plenty of open space and several willing participants – at least five, but probably no more than twenty.

Use a *Decider* from pages 8 to 13 to choose the chaser, known as 'It', 'He', or 'On'. Alternatively, the person who says *'Bags [baggy, or bagsy] me It!'* before anyone else is It.

All the players scatter, while It chases after them, trying to touch, or 'tag' someone, by tapping them on the shoulder.

Anyone tagged instantly becomes It. There is a rule that anyone who is tagged cannot immediately tag back the person who got them – they must go after someone else. The game ends when the last person is caught, or as soon as dinner is ready.

The game itself has any number of versions as well as names – just a few are detailed on the following pages.

Chain Tag
(Chainy)

Chain Tag requires good co-operation between the players for a successful chase. The smaller the space, the harder it is to escape from the chain!

How To Play

It begins the game as described on page 62, but when a player is tagged they must hold hands with It and continue the chase together. As more players are tagged the chain grows and grows, but a tag only counts if the whole chain is connected at the time of tagging.

If you get cornered, duck under the arms of two players in the chain and escape to freedom behind them.

Be the last to be tagged to win the game.

In a speedier version of *Chain Tag* players keep tagging until there are four people in the chain. The chain then splits into two pairs to chase down everyone else.

Tail Tag

A fun version of *Tag* for younger children, *Tail Tag* begins with all the players joined in a long 'snake', one behind the other.

If there are more than seven or eight people, divide into two groups to play. The person at the front must lead everyone around, trying to tag the last person in the snake's tail. Once tagged, the person at the back becomes the leader.

Stick In The Mud
(Freeze Tag)

Stick In The Mud is an energetic game that challenges children's flexibility and balance as well as their speed. It's best played on the grass as crawling on the ground is required.

How To Play

This is a variation on original *Tag* (see page 62). One person is chosen to be It, which means they must chase the other players in order to 'tag' them. It runs up as close as possible to another player and uses either hand to reach out and touch (rather than hit) them.

That person must then stand still with their legs and arms apart, as if they were frozen. Players who have not been tagged are able to 'free' a frozen person simply by crawling between their legs – easy does it though, so no one gets knocked off their feet!

The aim of the game is to avoid being the last person unfrozen or you will become It for the next game.

Tactical Tip

If you are not It, help the other players to remain free for as long as possible.

If you are It, try to tag all of the other players as quickly as you can. Tag people who are getting a little too close to freeing 'frozen' players first.

Crusts And Crumbs
(Rats And Rabbits or Soldiers And Sailors)

This ancient chasing game is played with two teams, but begins without either side having any idea if they are the hunting or being hunted.

How To Play

You need between six and twelve people to play. Divide into two teams, and select one person to act as 'Caller' (this

is a good role for an adult to play as they do not take part in the game and can act as an umpire at the same time).

Traditionally *Crusts And Crumbs* would have been played in the middle of the road, with the pavement on either side being the safe areas.

Playing in the park or playground is probably a more suitable alternative. Use bags and jumpers to mark out each end of a centre line with a safety line four to five metres away on either side.

The two teams line up to face each other about a metre apart at the centre line, with one team as 'Crusts', the other as 'Crumbs'.

When both teams are ready the Caller shouts out *'Crusts!'* or *'Crumbs!'*, either drawing out the beginning of the word to keep the suspense, or yelling the word suddenly to surprise everyone.

Whichever team is called is the chasing team, and must pursue the other team to their pavement or safe area.

Any player who is tagged switches to the opposing side until one team has caught all the members of the other team.

Twos And Threes
(Three Deep)

This is a tagging game that works well indoors, if space allows.

How To Play

You need an even number of players, six being an absolute minimum. Start by getting into twos – one person behind the other – and stand in a circle with everyone facing the centre.

Select one pair to go first, with the player on the outside being It and chasing the person in front.

If you are being chased you are able to run wherever you like, in and around the circle, and can escape tagging simply by stopping at the front of another pair, making a three.

At that moment It has to leave you alone and begin chasing after the player at the back of the three.

Anyone tagged becomes It instead, and immediately starts to race after the person who tagged them.

Shadow Tag

A non-contact version of traditional *Tag, Shadow Tag* has one vital ingredient – sunshine.

Players are tagged if It can stand on their shadow, so it's best to play in the afternoon when shadows are longer. One key rule is that participants are not allowed to pause for any length of time in the shade.

Kiss Chase

This is always a favourite for players of a 'certain age', but is often quite revolting to younger children in a mixed group because the single objective is to kiss each person you tag.

Capture The Flag
(French And English)

This exhilarating strategy game can be played with many people over a large area. It's ideal if you happen to be on a woodland picnic, but works well on a football pitch or in a park, too. You need two flags on sticks, made from old tea towels or any other spare pieces of fabric.

How To Play

Select two teams, and two territories, equal in size. This could simply be the two halves of a football pitch, or may involve dividing up the area of woodland or field where you are playing.

Each team chooses a base where they will keep any prisoners, then takes a flag, placing it securely within their territory.

The aim is to capture your enemy's flag, while defending your own. Teams can send individual members across or go in a big group, but if caught, players can be tagged and taken prisoner by the opposing team.

A team cannot capture the enemy flag again until they have freed all their players by reaching the enemy base and tagging them.

Tactical Tips

It helps to think strategically when placing your flag. It must be difficult to reach (without being dangerous) and you need to be able to see enemy players on the advance to defend the spot well.

Hide And Seek

A simple game of *Hide And Seek* is perfect to play with smaller children and can be enjoyed indoors or out as long as the area of play is established before you start.

How To Play

The Hiders run off to get settled in suitable nooks and crannies, while the Seeker counts to 100, possibly with hands over eyes and facing a corner for good measure. When finished counting the Seeker shouts, *'Coming, ready or not!'* before setting off to find everyone.

The first player to be found is the next Seeker; the last person to be found is the winner of that game.

Sardines

Sardines is a fun variation on *Hide And Seek*, usually played indoors, unless there are the right sort of hiding places available outside.

How To Play

Unlike traditional *Hide And Seek*, in *Sardines* one person goes off to hide, while all the other players count to 100, then split up to search. The key difference is that once a Seeker finds the Hider, they must join him or her in the hiding spot. The smaller the space chosen to hide, the more squashed up everyone will eventually be, until the last person discovers all the sardines.

Tactical Tip

Keep a close eye on your fellow Seekers. If a Seeker goes off to part of the house but doesn't return, there's a good chance that they have found the hiding place.

Block
(Kickstone One, Two, Three)

Block is an energetic variation on the classic *Hide And Seek* theme. The Seeker not only tries to find the Hiders, but has to race them back to the starting-point, known as the 'block'. The block, or 'kickstone', was traditionally a lamp post or bollard, but it could just as easily be a tree or step.

How To Play

The Seeker covers their eyes and counts to 100. The rest of the players scatter and hide. Then the hunting begins.

On spotting someone, the Seeker runs back to touch the block and shouts *'Block'* or *'Kickstone one, two, three, I spy [Name]'* inserting the name of the person spotted. They are then out or 'blocked'.

For Hiders, the aim is to get back to the block before the Seeker, shouting *'One, two, three, block home,'* or *'Kickstone one, two, three'*.

The game continues until either everyone is home free, or blocked. The person who was caught first becomes the Seeker for the next game.

Word And Memory Games

Set yourself a mental challenge with this selection
of the best mind-bending games ever.

I Spy

This is a classic game of observation and cunning, perfect for filling time on a boring car journey and just as good for long, hot afternoons in summer. Can you spot something that no one else can?

How To Play

Choose someone to begin the game – very often this is the person whose idea it was to play. The starting player secretly selects an object that everyone can see, before saying:

'I spy with my little eye, something beginning with (letter)'

naming the letter that their object begins with.

The other players then look around for any possible objects beginning with that letter and take turns to guess what it is.

Logic is paramount here. If you are playing in a car it's important that the object you pick is not left far behind you on the motorway. For instance, don't pick B for Bridge unless you are stuck in a long queue of traffic. Your chosen object will soon become a distant speck behind you. The first person to successfully guess the object gets to choose the next *I Spy*.

Tactical Tips

Consider the skill levels of your opponents. It's easier and quicker to pick something obvious, but spend a few moments planning ahead to make it as difficult as you can for the other players.

If you're playing against a particularly cunning opponent keep an eye on their line of sight while they're choosing and while you guess the object. Just how deceptive are they?

Alphabet Minute

Alphabet Minute is played in teams of two, with as many pairs as you want. You'll just need paper and pencils for everyone and a watch or clock to time people with.

How To Play

Before the game starts, everyone writes down a simple topic of conversation on a slip of paper, such as the weather, or television, along with a letter of the alphabet.

The papers are then folded and put into a hat or bowl.

The first team picks out a paper and looks at the subject they have chosen and the letter of the alphabet specified. They must then strike up a conversation on that subject, for 60 seconds.

The opening sentence has to begin with the specified letter and subsequent sentences must begin with the following letters of the alphabet in sequence, until the speaker gets back to the letter they began with or the 60 seconds is up.

Here's an example:

Topic: Television
Letter: T

'The news is my favourite programme on television.'
'Unbelievable, are you sure?'
'Vital to having brilliant general knowledge though.'
'Why? I'd rather play a game.'
'X-ray research shows it's good for you.'
'You're really strange.'
'Zany is a better word.'

The winning team is the one who gets round the alphabet fastest, or who goes furthest in 60 seconds.

Fizz Buzz

This game is a great test of mental agility and an excellent way to pass the time on a long journey.

It can just be a fun participation game, but you can add a competitive element by punishing mistakes with losses of 'lives', or paying forfeits.

How To Play

Contestants must take turns to count up from one to 100.

Each time you would usually say the number three, a number divisible by three, or a number that has a three in it, you must say 'Fizz' instead.

At the same time, whenever you would usually say the number seven, a number divisible by seven, or a number that has a seven in it, say 'Buzz' instead.

If a number is divisible by both three and seven or has a three and a seven in it, you must say 'Fizz Buzz':

'One, two, Fizz, four, five, Fizz, Buzz, eight, Fizz, ten, eleven,
Fizz, Fizz, Buzz, Fizz, sixteen, Buzz, Fizz, nineteen, twenty,
Fizz Buzz,' and so on.

Every time a player accidentally says a number rather than
Fizz, Buzz or Fizz Buzz they use up a life or must pay a
forfeit. Once everyone has taken a turn and reached 100,
the player who has lost fewest lives is the winner.

Tactical Tip

For a simpler version use just 'Fizz'
for threes, or 'Buzz' for sevens. This
can easily be a game in itself,
especially for younger players, or
can be used to practise for the full
knockout Fizz Buzz version.

I Went To Market

This is a fantastic game to sharpen your memory, sure to give you the giggles as you think up weirder items to buy. *I Went To Market* is perfect for younger players learning the alphabet as well as improving their memory skills.

How To Play

Players take turns to suggest the items bought at market in alphabetical order saying *'I went to market and I bought...'* The first person begins with the letter A – *'some apples'* for example – then the second person repeats *'apples'* before adding something of their own, beginning with the letter B. They should say *'I went to market and bought some apples and some bread.'* The third player repeats the items beginning with A and B and adds another beginning with C and so on. Agree beforehand if you think everyone should be allowed to pass over difficult letters like X and Z.

You can play the game with genuine market items such as apples and bread if you prefer, or let players use their imagination to buy anything and everything under the sun. If you get stuck on a particular letter, or you can't remember the complete sequence, you lose a life. Three misses and you're out.

Kim's Game

Kim's Game is a great way to test your powers of recall. The beauty of the game is that it's played with household objects, so it's just a question of using whatever you might have to hand at home.

How To Play

One person gathers together a selection of 15 to 20 household objects and places them on a tray. Smaller items, such as a pen, a cotton reel, an apple, or a marble, are ideal.

Players have one minute to study and memorise the items before the tray is covered with a cloth.

Each player has a piece of paper and a pen to write down as many of the items as they can remember. A point is scored for each item remembered correctly, but a point is lost for any that were never there (it does happen!). The highest scoring player wins.

You can play *Kim's Game* as a single round or over several rounds, allowing different players to set the challenge. With regular practice players can increase the number of items to remember and reduce the time allowed to memorise them.

Singing And Circle Games

A good sing-song is always popular so gather round and put your heart and voice into these childhood favourites.

The Farmer's In His Den
(The Farmer's In The Dell)

This popular singing game is ideal for between 10 and 12 players, but more people can join in if space allows.

How To Play

Gather everyone into a circle. One player is chosen to be the 'Farmer' who stands in the middle of the circle, or the 'den'. The players dance around the Farmer and sing:

> *'The farmer's in his den,*
> *The farmer's in his den,*
> *Ee-aye-addio,*
> *The farmer's in his den*
>
> *The farmer wants a wife,*
> *The farmer wants a wife,*
> *Ee-aye-addio,*
> *The farmer wants a wife.'*

At this point the Farmer selects a 'wife' from the circle. She goes to stand with him in the centre and everyone sings:

> *The wife wants a child,*
> *The wife wants a child,*

Ee-aye-addio,
The wife wants a child.'

The child wants a nurse,
The child wants a nurse,
Ee-aye-addio,
The child wants a nurse.'

The nurse wants a dog,
The nurse wants a dog,
Ee-aye-addio,
The nurse wants a dog.'

We all pat the dog,
We all pat the dog,
Ee-aye-addio,
We all pat the dog.'

On each verse a person is selected to
join the family in the centre.

When the 'dog' has been chosen everyone
sings 'We all pat the dog', crowding around
to pat the dog.

Oranges And Lemons

Oranges And Lemons is a well-known children's song, dating from 1744, which describes the sounds of the church bells in and around the City of London. The words have altered over the years and here is the song we know so well today:

> 'Oranges and Lemons,'
> *Say the bells of St Clement's,*
>
> 'You owe me five farthings,'
> *Say the bells of St Martin's,*
>
> 'When will you pay me?'
> *Say the bells of Old Bailey,*
>
> 'When I grow rich,'
> *Say the bells of Shoreditch,*
>
> 'When will that be?'
> *Say the bells of Stepney,*
>
> 'I do not know,'
> *Says the great bell at Bow.*
>
> *Here comes a candle*
> *to light you to bed.*
> *Here comes a chopper*
> *to chop off your head!*
>
> *Chip-chop, chip-chop,*
> *The last man's DEAD!*

How To Play

Two players decide in secret which of them is *'Oranges'* and which is *'Lemons'*. Then they form an arch with both hands. The rest of the players dance, walk or run through the arch while singing the rhyme.

On *'Chip-chop, chip-chop, the last man's DEAD'*
the children forming the arch drop their arms and
capture a player. They ask their victim to choose
to be Oranges or Lemons. Their victim whispers
the answer and then stands behind
the appropriate person.

The game continues until everyone is caught and
two lines have formed. Then the Oranges and
Lemons engage in a 'ropeless' tug-of-war, with
everyone holding onto the waist of the child in
front and attempting to pull the opposing team
over to their side.

92

In And Out
The Dusty Bluebells

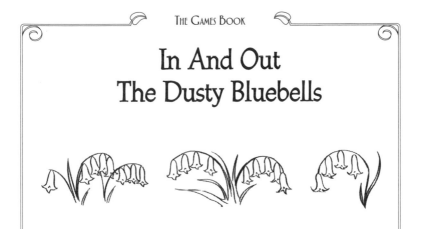

This is a great game for sunny days in the garden or playground, and needs 10 or 12 people to work well.

How To Play

Everyone except It stands in a circle holding hands, raising their arms to make arches. It then skips around the circle, in and out of each arch, while everyone sings:

> *In and out the dusty bluebells,*
> *In and out the dusty bluebells,*
> *In and out the dusty bluebells,*
> *Who shall be the leader?*
>
> *Tip tap, tip tap on your shoulder,*
> *Tip tap, tip tap on your shoulder,*
> *Tip tap, tip tap on your shoulder,*
> *You shall be the leader.*

As the first verse finishes It stops and taps the nearest player on the shoulder. The person tapped unlinks themself from the circle, grabs It around the waist from behind, and allows themself to be led in and out of the arches while the song begins again. Each time the second verse is sung another player is added to the back of the chain. For added emphasis each player in the chain can tap the person in front on the shoulder at the same time.

Knots

This game will get everyone into a terrible tangle and back again. You'll need at least ten people for it to work well.

How To Play

With an even number of players standing in a circle, each person puts out their left hand and holds hands with another left hand. Everyone repeats with their right hand, but with a different person.

Now carefully unravel yourselves back into a circle. It's much harder than it sounds!

In A Ravel

For a more chaotic version, everyone forms a line and holds hands with the person either side of them. The first in line dips between two arms, or crawls under someone's legs, bringing the whole line with them like a bizarre version of *Follow My Leader*.

Without letting go of each other's hands everyone continues weaving in and out until they are all tied up in a huge knot. The last player in line has to untangle the knot without anyone letting go of their neighbour's hand.

Duck, Duck, Goose

This chasing game requires the ability to run fast in a circle rather than a straight line. The more people involved the merrier, but the further you'll have to run!

How To Play

Everyone sits in a large circle, facing inwards. One person is selected as Goose and walks slowly around, touching each player gently on the head, saying 'Duck' each time. When the time is right the Goose touches the next person on the head and suddenly shouts 'Goose!'

That player must jump up and chase the Goose around the circle – be ready for a sprint! If the Goose gets round to the empty space before being tagged they become a Duck and sit down, and the loser becomes the Goose.

Tactical Tip

Choose your Duck wisely. Select someone who isn't paying much attention as you pass. Be ready to run as soon as you shout 'Goose!' to get a good head start on your opponent.

Ball Games

The perfect combination of good fun,
great exercise and skill, ball games are sure to
exhaust even the most competitive child.

Queenie

This is a very simple game to play, as long as you can keep a straight face. It's at least a hundred years old and, despite the name, it's just as much fun for boys to play as it is for girls! It's best played with a small ball, such as a tennis ball, which will be easy to hide, and with a minumum of four or five players.

How To Play

Select one player to be 'Queenie' and line up in a row behind her. Queenie tosses the ball over her shoulder, without looking, and the other players immediately rush for the ball. Once one player has the ball everyone except Queenie should line up again with their hands behind their backs and chant:

> *'Queenie, Queenie, who's got the ball?*
> *I haven't got it; it isn't in my pocket,*
> *Queenie, Queenie who's got the ball?'*

Queenie must then turn around and try to guess which other player has the ball behind their back. If she guesses correctly Queenie plays again, otherwise the person with the ball takes over.

Tactical Tip

If you do get hold of the ball, remember not to give yourself away by crying out in excitement. It's also vital to have a good 'poker' face so that Queenie doesn't suspect you.

If you are Queenie, keep an eye out for giggling faces and shaking shoulders — they are sure to lead you straight to the person with the ball.

Kingy

This traditional ball game is a quick and skilful challenge for 10 to 15 competitors. Use a small, bouncy ball and play within a tennis court or playground so that it will be stopped by walls or fences if it goes astray.

How To Play

First choose a Chaser – if you suggested the game this is a good excuse to elect yourself. Start by bouncing the ball ten times, giving the others a chance to spread out.

Get players out and onto your side by hitting them with the ball, aimed only between the shoulders and knees. You cannot run with the ball but can dribble it, bouncing it along the ground as you run to get close enough to aim.

Players who are hit correctly have to help you chase and throw, but once there are two or more people chasing, you are no longer allowed to move with the ball at all. Instead, you can throw the ball across to each other to cover more ground.

Defending players can ward the ball off by knocking it away with a clenched fist. However, if the ball is caught by a Chaser before it bounces, that player is out. The ball cannot be kicked or touched, other than with clenched fists, but gripping it between two fists to throw it out of the Chasers' reach is permitted. If players are tagged while holding the ball they are also out.

The last player left is 'King', and is allowed to decide who the next Chaser will be.

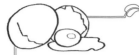

Bad Eggs

This popular game combines a good memory with running, ball-catching and throwing skills.

How To Play

You'll need a tennis ball and an open space with around six to eight players – any more makes it difficult to remember everyone's identity. Choose a category such as colours, days of the week (as long as the number of players is not more than seven) or simply numbers. Assign a colour, day or number to each player.

One player starts with the ball and throws it up in the air, calling out one of the colours or days of the week at the same time. If your colour is called you must run in to catch the ball, while everyone else tries to get as far away as possible.

When the ball is caught shout 'Stop!' to make everyone freeze. Take three giant strides towards another player, and throw the ball, attempting to hit them below the knee. A hit gives that player one 'Bad Egg', or penalty point, for the next round – a miss and you get the Bad Egg.

Three Bad Eggs and you're out.
Someone else then gets the ball
to start the game again.

Tactical Tip

Sometimes rolling the ball along the
ground can be easier and more
accurate than throwing – although a
lot of the fun of the game is in
throwing the ball as hard as possible.
Just don't be surprised if you get the
same treatment!

French Cricket

A simplified version of cricket for the beach or park, the
only equipment necessary is a tennis ball and an old bat.
Obviously a cricket bat is perfect, but an old tennis racquet
or rounders bat will be fine, too.

How To Play

As long as there are more than three of you, any number of
people can play. In *French Cricket* there is just one batsman
while everyone else fields and bowls. The ball can only be
bowled underarm and the batsman's legs must act as wicket.

The starting batsman stands in the middle of the playing
area, with one fielder ready to bowl from a reasonable
distance. The aim is to hit the batsman's legs, below the
knee, or catch the ball before it bounces – both knock out
the batsman, giving you the chance to bat instead.

The batsman is not allowed to move his feet and defends his
legs with the bat. He scores a run by passing the bat around
his body until a fielder gets the ball and bowls it back again.

Once you have all batted, the player with most runs wins.

Sevens

Challenge others or just yourself in this brilliant ball game, increasing in difficulty the further you progress. It can take hours to complete and years to perfect.

How To Play

Find a tennis ball and a flat, outside wall. Stand about two metres from the wall and follow the directions for each stage below:

- Throw the ball at the wall and catch it.
- Hit the wall, let it bounce, catch it.
- Hit the wall, swat the ball back with the palm of your hand and catch it.
- Hit the wall, swat it back at the wall, let it bounce once and catch it.
- Hit the wall, bounce once, bounce it again with the palm of your hand and catch it.

- Hit the wall, swat it back at the wall, bounce once, bounce it again with your hand and catch it.
- Hit the wall, swat it back at the wall, let it bounce, bounce it again, swat it back at the wall and catch it.

When you have mastered these moves begin again, adding the following variations on each manoeuvre:

- Clap your hands each time you throw the ball.
- Clap your hands twice after throwing the ball.
- Spin around each time you throw the ball.
- Go through each stage using only your right hand.
- Now do each stage using just your left hand.
- Start each stage by throwing the ball under your right leg.
- Now try each stage throwing the ball under your left leg.

If all that is just too easy you can combine as many skill variations as you like then challenge a friend to a *Sevens* championship match.

String, Cards And Paper Games

For a dozen completely absorbing ways to fill rainy days
and holidays, you need only the most basic supplies.

Cat's Cradle

This compulsive string game for two will keep you occupied for hours on end.

How To Play

Tie a 160 cm piece of string into a loop. Then put both hands, except the thumbs, inside the loop and wrap it around each hand again. With your middle finger hook the string which lies across the opposite palm from underneath and pull. Repeat with the other hand to make 'Cat's Cradle' (1).

A Soldier's Bed

Using both thumbs and index fingers, your partner should nip the Cat's Cradle from above at the two points where the strings criss-cross (2). They then pull the

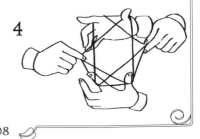

crosses around the outside strings and scoop them up through the centre. Let the Cradle go so that your partner can pull it taut (3).

Candles

In exactly the same way, grip the two points on the Soldier's Bed where the long strings intersect (4). Scoop them around and up through the centre. As you draw the strings apart they will form four parallel lines (5).

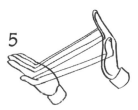

Manger

Using both little fingers, your partner now hooks the inside string next to your index finger and the inside string next your thumb, pulling them out to make a square (6). Your partner then scoops up the outside strings with both thumbs and index fingers making a reverse Cradle (7).

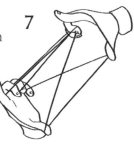

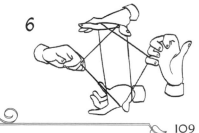

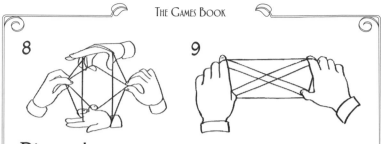

Diamonds

In the same way your partner made the Soldier's Bed, bring the crosses around the outside strings (8), but instead go down into the centre, before pulling taut (9).

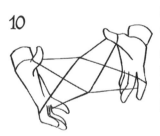

Cat's Eyes

Your partner then repeats the actions you used to make Candles, but a pattern of four triangles is mysteriously created instead (10).

Fish In A Dish

Now put your thumbs and index fingers down into each of the triangles, scoop up through the centre and pull out to make your Fish In A Dish (11).

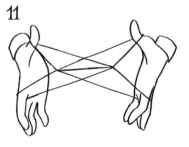

Snap

Perfect for beginners, *Snap* is a great game for kids, who will love its nail-biting nature. Quick reflexes are essential, and remember, shouting loudest doesn't mean you're first!

How To Play

Snap can be played between just two players, or several. Use an extra pack of cards if more than four people are playing.

Deal the cards out among players as evenly as possible. Players should keep their cards piled face down in front of them. The player on the dealer's left begins, turning their top card face-up and creating a new central stack.

Players take turns placing a card on the central stack, keeping watch for a card matching the one underneath it. When this happens, the first to shout *'Snap!'* takes all the cards in the central pile and adds them to the bottom of his or her stack.

The next player to the left continues the game. Players are only out of the game when their stack runs out. *Snap* champion is the player who wins all the cards in play.

Slapjack

Fast, furious and even a little physical, this card game is a great kids' favourite and ideal for two to four players.

How To Play

The dealer shuffles the pack then deals all 52 cards in a clockwise direction, starting with the player to the left.

Players hold their cards face-down in the palm of one hand, but do not look at them. The person to the left of the dealer begins, turning their top-most card up and placing it in the centre. Play continues in dealing order.

Everyone watches carefully for a Jack to appear and tries to be the first to slap a hand over the Jack – 'Slapjack' – to win the cards in the centre pile. Those cards are then added to the bottom of the pile in their hand and the game continues with the next player to the left.

If a player loses all their cards to the other players, they can still stay in the game. They should count the Jacks and when three have gone, pay extra attention to make sure they are the first to Slapjack. When one player has all the cards, the game is over.

Patience
(Solitaire)

An excellent solo card game to help long Sundays go by, this is one of the commonest versions of *Patience*.

How To Play

Shuffle a pack of cards then deal seven cards face-down in a row. Deal a second card on each pile except the first, then a third card on each pile except the first two and so on, so that the seventh pile has seven cards. This row forms your main *Patience* layout. Turn the top card of each pile over and keep the remaining cards face-down in a single stack.

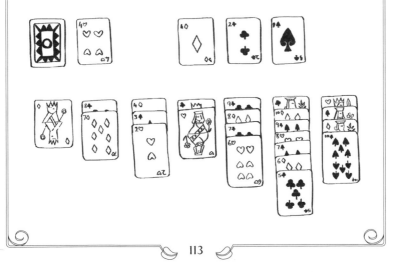

Cards on the main layout can be moved to sit below the next highest card of the opposite colour. When a card has been moved, turn over the face-down card just uncovered.

Build up runs of cards on the main layout in alternating colour order from high to low values. When you come across Aces, start four individual 'foundation' piles above the main layout. Your aim is to add cards of the same suit in ascending order from Ace to King to these foundation piles as they are revealed in the main layout.

If you find you cannot move any cards, use the stack of spare cards to help move the game along. Turn over each card in the pile one by one and if you can place it in one of the columns do. If you cannot, discard it in a face-up pile, keeping the top-most card free to play.

When one of the seven columns becomes empty can move a King, or a run starting with a King, into the gap.

Tactical Tip

It's sensible not to move cards to the foundation piles too soon as, once there, they cannot be moved. You may need certain cards later to allow the game to continue.

Clock Patience

This is a classic *Patience* game played in a circular pattern.

How To Play

Deal twelve cards face-down
in a pattern that mimics the
numbers on a clock face with
another card in the centre of
your 'clock'. Repeat until you
have four cards in each pile.

To start, turn over the top card on the centre pile. This
directs you to one of the piles on the clock face. Aces are at
one o'clock, twos are at two o'clock, right round to Queens
at twelve o'clock.

Place your card under the pile or beside it. Turn over the
top card of this pile to find out where to go to next.

Whenever you turn over a King, you must place it in the
centre and take a card from the centre pile to start again.
The aim is to turn over all the cards in the twelve piles, but
once you have revealed all four Kings the game is over.

Rummy

Rummy makes for a perfect family game as children can easily compete against adults.

How To Play

For two players, deal ten cards each. Three to four players get seven cards each, and five to six have six cards each. The rest of the pack is placed in a face-down stack, and the top card is turned face-up next to it.

The aim of the game is to be the first player to get rid of all their cards. Cards can be disguarded if they can be grouped into 'melds' – three or four of a kind – or 'runs' – three or more cards of the same suit in order (note that Aces are low).

So when players look at their hand they should start to organise the cards into these groups.

Play Begins

The person to the left of the dealer begins, choosing to pick up either the face-up card in the centre or the unknown card from the top of the stack. They must

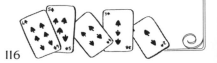

then place one unwanted card from their hand face-up on the 'discard' pile.

If the player can already make a run or meld, now is the time to lay it down, face-up on the table, before the next person takes their turn.

If another player holds any cards that match a meld or run that has been placed on the table, they can lay these cards down when it comes to their turn.

The winner of the round is the first to lay down all their cards. The value of the other player's remaining cards are added up to make the winner's score. Kings, Queens and Jacks count for ten points, Aces one point – the remaining cards are valued as the number on the card.

Play continues until one player reaches 100 points and wins the whole game.

Tactical Tips

Try to avoid taking cards from the discard pile as this will alert other players to the cards you are hoping for.

Beetle

A simple dice game for two or more people, players must compete to complete their beetle first.

How To Play

Each person has paper and a pencil. Players take turns to roll the dice and the person scoring the highest number starts the game. Play then moves in a clockwise direction. Everyone must roll a six before they are allowed to draw the beetle's head. Only then can they draw the rest of the beetle, although the other body parts can be added in any order. Roll:

- One for each of the Beetle's two wings.
- Two for its tail.
- Three for each of its antennae.
- Four for each of the two eyes.
- Five for each of the six legs.
- Six for the Beetle's head.

As soon as your creepy crawly is done shout *'Beetle!'* to stop the game and claim victory.

Consequences

This makes an excellent game for rainy days and quiet evenings. Up to eight people can play – you just need enough paper and pencils for everyone.

How To Play

Each person writes down the name of a boy, then folds their piece of paper over before passing it to the left. On the next line everyone writes:

met [inserting the name of a girl]
and folds and passes the paper along.
Each player then adds:
in/at [the name of a place].
Then everyone describes the clothes the girl was wearing.
The next person must write down the clothes that the boy was wearing, then:
He [each person writes down what the boy did].
Then she [everyone should describe what the girl did]
before switching to write:
He said...
Then: *she said...* and finally:
The consequences were...

When the paper is unfolded it might read:

'Jack met Carrie at the roller-disco. Carrie was wearing pink jeans and a green cardigan with sequins. Jack was wearing his school uniform. He got hiccups. Then she did a cartwheel. He said "There's a fly in my soup." She said "Where did you get that hat?". The consequences were that the rain ruined the barbecue.'

Each time you write a line of the story you'll be completely unaware of the previous element so the consequences can be quite bizarre. Your stories could be even funnier if the characters involved are people that you all know, or well-known celebrities.

Picture Perfect

As an alternative try *Picture Consequences*. The object of the game is to collectively draw a person, with the funniest results possible. Paper and pencils, plus colouring pens if you like, are the only equipment necessary.

How To Play

Divide the paper into several sections depending on the number of players. First draw a head and neck, then fold the paper over so that it can't be seen except for the bottom of the neck. This will indicate to the next player where they should continue. They then draw the chest, shoulders and arms, and fold the paper over before handing it on. The next player draws the whole lower part of the body, down to the knees. Finally, the last player draws the lower legs, feet and shoes.

Tactical Tips

The more gruesome and exaggerated the features and clothing you draw, the funnier it will be – express yourselves! Once you've all got the hang of it, you can suggest titles for your pictures, such as 'The man you'll marry', or 'What our geography teacher looks like'.

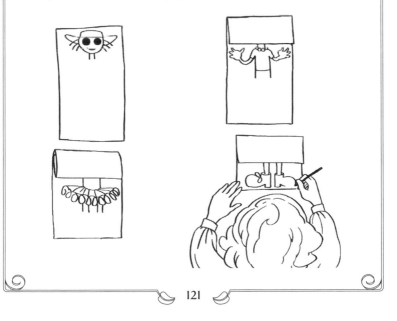

Hangman

A reliable favourite for a quiet afternoon indoors, *Hangman* is a classic word game for two or more players. You'll need to hold your nerve as the gallows is built while you try to guess your opponent's word.

How To Play

Think of a word and mark down dashes for the number of letters it has on a piece of paper. The other player must guess the word by suggesting letters. If they guess a letter correctly, write it on the appropriate dash.

Each time their guess is wrong, add another piece of the gallows! Start with the base, then a vertical strut, a diagonal cross-piece, the horizontal arm, a diagonal section to hold it up, followed by the rope.

There are six more chances for your opponent to work out the word – the head, body, two arms and two legs.

Tactical Tip

Certain letters of the alphabet occur more often than others so guess the most common letters first: e, s, a, t.

Noughts And Crosses
(Tic-tac-toe)

Possibly the simplest tactical game ever, *Noughts And Crosses* is still a highly competitive way to keep busy.

How To Play

Draw a grid of four intersecting lines – two vertical, two horizontal – making nine small squares. Choose Noughts or Crosses then toss a coin to see who will start.

Your aim is to get three Noughts or three Crosses in a line, horizontally, vertically or diagonally. To start, draw your 'X' or 'O' on any one of the nine spaces. Your opponent can then draw in their piece, concentrating on how to block your next move as well as trying to start a row of their own.

Nine Men's Morris
(Merels or Mills)

Nine Men's Morris is an ancient board game for two people. It can easily be played using paper and pencil to draw up a board with coins or draughts pieces as the 'Men'.

How To Play

Draw three concentric squares and mark the corners and halfway points of each with a dot. Link the halfway points with vertical and horizontal lines.

Gather nine Men each, whether bottle tops, buttons, pebbles or coins, as long as they differ from your opponent's. Decide who will start and take turns to place your Men on empty dots on the board.

Once all the pieces are on the board, take turns to move them to adjacent points, aiming to line up three Men, either horizontally or vertically, in a row called a 'mill'.

Each time you are successful, you can remove any one of your opponent's Men from the board, as long as it is not already part of a mill.

If your opponent moves two Men into a line, try to get to a blocking position to prevent them adding a third.

When your opponent is unable to move any of their Men or has only two pieces left, you are the winner.

An extra rule in some versions allows players to move pieces anywhere on the board, regardless of lines, if they are reduced to just three Men. Decide whether to play by this rule before the game begins.

Tactical Tip

Aim to set up two safe mills, which your opponent cannot reach. Switch between the two to keep making mills, reducing your opponent's Men.

ALSO AVAILABLE:
The Nursery Rhyme Book: £5.00
ISBN: 978-1-84317-307-6

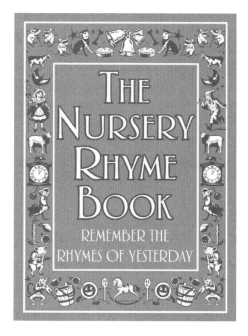

If you would like to order this book please contact:
Bookpost, PO Box 29, Douglas, Isle of Man, IM99 1BQ
Tel. 01624 677237 Fax 01624 670923